Make a Funny Face

Christine Finochio • Jennette MacKenzie

Make a big circle.

Cut it out.

Make two little triangles.

Cut them out.

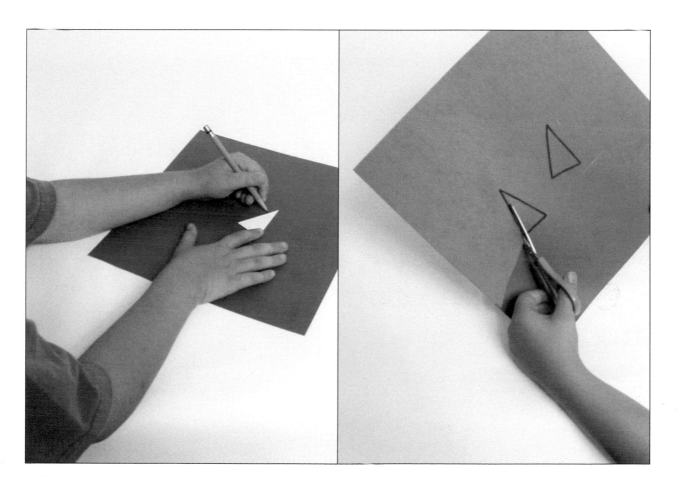

Glue   the   eyes.

Make a little square.

Cut it out.

Glue the nose.

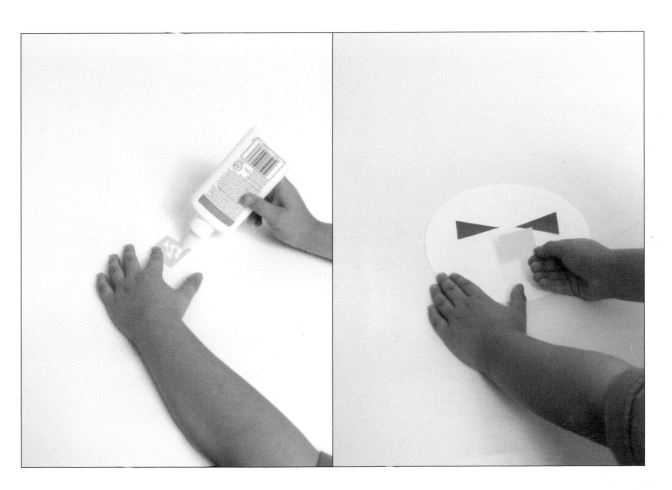

Make a rectangle.

Cut it out.

Glue the mouth.

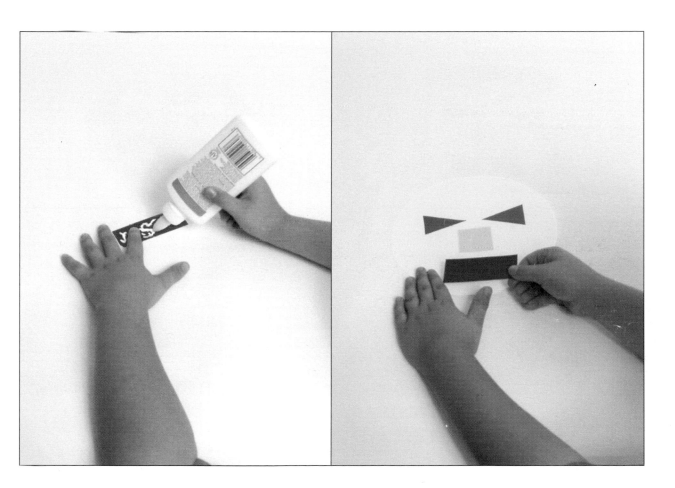

Can you make the hair?